In Case You Were Wondering

A Portrait of Life

MICHAEL LOYD ROGERS

In Case You Were Wondering: A Portrait of Life
Copyright © 2022 by Michael Loyd Rogers

All rights reserved under international and Pan-American copyright conventions. No part of this book may be reproduced, stored in a retrieval system, or transmitted in any form, electronic, mechanical, or by other means, without written permission of the author.

ISBN: 979-8-9859688-1-1

Sregor
Houston, TX
docr4@sbcglobal.net

Design by Sarah Katreen Hoggatt of BookLayoutBiz.com

Following Illustrations/Photo-Art provided by:

Michael L. Rogers
   Reflections (Photo-Art)
   Future Shock (Oil Painting)
   But I Was Afraid (Photo-Art)
   Missing You (Drawing)
   Sometimes Go By (Drawing)

Kareem Y. Rogers
   Where I Live (Photo-Art)
   Guilty Until Proven Innocent (Drawing)
   The Event (Drawing)
   Things Said (Drawing)

Naomi Gatt
   Continuing Thoughts (Watercolor)

Contents

Acknowledgments	v
Forward	1
A Letter to Myself	5
The Main Ingredient	6
Reflections	9
Looking Into the Mirror	11
Where I Live	13
Friends	15
But We Keep On Goin Thru Changes!	17
Guilty Until Proven Innocent	18
Out Of The Closet Of My Mind	21
Future Shock	23
The Destiny of Man	25
Imagination	27
Imagining You Here	29
So Many Questions, Now Isn't That Strange?	31
The Woman In Red	33
My Muse	35
I Want To Know Your Name	36
The Blossom of Spring	39
My Heart Sings	41
The Event	43
You Mean The World To Me	45
I Can't Tell You Why	47
If I Give You My Heart, What Will You Do With It?	49
The Little Leaf that Fell to Love	50
Dwelling Thoughts	53
Continuing Thoughts	55

But I Was Afraid	57
Things Said	59
Make Up Your Mind	61
Running Away to Love	63
The Picture	65
Missing You	67
The Discovery	69
How Could I Have Ever Let You Go?	71
Back Together?	73
A Rose May Whither And Die	75
With This Ring	77
You Know, Sometimes Go By	79
The Land of Hummingbirdsand Butterflies	81
In Case You Were Wondering	83
The Author	85

Acknowledgments

Many thanks to the St. Louis, Globe Democrat for awarding their Essay Winner Award to "The Main Ingredient," published 1985.

I also thank Poetry.com and the International Library of Poetry for awarding their Editor's Choice Award to "So Many Questions, Now Isn't That Strange?," published in Forever Spoken by the International Library of Poetry 2007.

A special acknowledgment to my muses for their steadfast support and inspiration:

- **Gwendolyn Mann-Rogers**: Thank you Gwen, for being my inspiration as well as an encourager of my early artistic endeavors.
- **Sheryl Smith-Rogers**: Thank you Sheryl, for constantly pushing me to be and do my best and being an early supporter of my art and writing.
- **Loretta Smith (Mom)**: Thank you Mom, for loving me as a son, being a great role model, and always being there for me; whenever my world spun into chaos.
- **Linda Brown**: Thank you Linda, for always believing in me and being a great friend.
- **Emily Ottinger**: Thank you Emily, for being there and holding me up; when I needed support and a ray of hope in my life.
- **Tiana Lara**: Thank you Tiana, for inspiring a connective element to my writing; My friend forever; "the little leaf that fell to love."

I shall always be grateful that they were, and still are a part of my life; they helped me see, those things I could not see; "They all, made me want to be, that other side of me."

Forward

While riding the emotional rollercoaster of life, we sometimes find ourselves spinning around in life's orbit. We experience a multitude of emotional transitions, which give us cause to pause and reflect on our environment, our social-personal relationships, and primarily, ourselves. Although circumstances of our lives may vary, the human element of emotion impacts us all; regardless of gender or social status, the circle of life touches us all. It is the intensity of the emotional state that we don't always see.

This collection illustrates the search for the ever-elusive answers to life's questions related to our social-emotional state of well-being. Fantasies and imaginations continuously take us on emotional journeys that expose beginnings and endings in the circle of life. The impact to various states of wonder, joy, love, hope, pain and sorrow, take on new meaning once exposed for all to see; birthing the pros and cons of who we are and what we may or may not represent.

Becoming aware of who we are, ultimately brings us to a point of understanding that we are indeed, human, and that life waits for no man. It is at this juncture that one has to summon the courage to venture out into the orbiting world. Hopefully, we land still having love for others, as well as ourselves.

Life continues to rotate; circling back to you! The search for life's answers at the end of the rainbow still goes on. If you click your heels three times, you might end up in Kansas; but if you blink your eyes three times, you may very well land inside a portrait of life.

"In my youth I learned to be hard, but as I aged I learned to be gentle; even unto myself."

— Michael Loyd Rogers

"Art is a statement; be it social, political or personal. Sometimes it eludes the viewer, but the artist is definitely making a statement. If there exists a state of beauty, happiness, sadness or strife, it is the artist who exposes it for all to see. We exist in an environment that is very real and tangible; and reality at some point in ones existence should be confronted."

— Michael Loyd Rogers

"A voice can speak the story, but only the mind can tell the story."

— Michael Loyd Rogers

A Letter to Myself

Dear Me,

As life continues its forward path, you find yourself thinking increasingly about the reason for your being and who you are. Life has twisted and turned down many roads. It sometimes has gone full circle round and round. The birth of children, the deaths of your friends and elders; it is puzzling how life can be joy and happiness, with pain and suffering at the same time. A double-edged sword this thing called life certainly is. You have seen life and death pursue others and on more than one occasion, it had stared you in the face.

Life can be harsh, showing no favor to man, woman, or child. But sometimes harshness is required to hone you into a strengthened state of mind. Through it all you stayed the course. Your thoughts regained their clarity and revealed feelings never felt before; you felt love for yourself for the very first time.

There have been moments in your life where you thought you felt this way; moments of vanity and selfishness that led you to believe that you could not be duped or fooled. In those moments you had lied to yourself by trying to create or make love happen; even though it was not there. Simply because that, is what you wanted. Driven by your social conditioning, as well as your perceptions of what others would say, feel, or do relative to your choices in life; You now realize how life's disappointments can steal your joy if you let them. Well, you refuse to lie down, quit, or throw caution to the wind; and you refuse to (in this lifetime) not experience true love.

Love can carry you at times when you lack the strength to take just one more step. Love can make you smile and instill joy in you at even the darkest moments. Love can bless you with the powers of being. You feel at this moment in your life, after careful consideration, after weighing all the facts, after interrogating yourself under the hot lamp of life experiences; you have finally found a reason for being. You have unwittingly found love for yourself, while walking life's path. Yes, you found love, and love means the world to you. You also found that love has a name...loves name is You!

The Main Ingredient

The world balances on the brink of nuclear war. Our offspring suffer an underlying fear that their inherent right to the pursuit of happiness may be denied. Free enterprise is not so free anymore, just ask your local small businessman. Self-reliance is becoming trendy because your neighbor looks the other way. Family life, once the way of life, and the staunch moral values that accompanied it have been ushered into the closet. The new moral values that this society has incubated; have now hatched into promiscuity, battered wives, abused children, an accelerating suicide rate, the list could go on and on. Why is this all happening?

This decay of our moral attitudes is due to the abolishment of religious values. It seems that religion has been swept under the carpet. There once was a time when religion was the main ingredient in the home. Religion tended to bring and keep the family together; it taught us to share, to be morally upright; and most of all, it taught us to love one another and to love and respect our fellow man. It is more love that this society needs; the love of God and those with whom we co-exist.

Everything that God and religion stand for is being discriminated against and shut out at every turn. Religion is being shut out of our very lives; our schools (public prayer is taboo), our homes, and even our churches. More and more, churches are leaning toward materialism, dabbling in real estate, squeezing into the financial arenas and politics. What has happened to religion? Where has it gone?

Religion is still in existence (there are a few hangers-on), but fast falling by the wayside. It is over-shadowed by our ever-growing materialistic society whose motto is becoming, "it's not what's in your heart, but what's in your bank account"; or better still, "Divided we stand and United we fall." Without religion in our society, we will all surely fall, for it is knowledge of religion that can offer our society hope:

- Hope, that family life will again come into vogue.
- Hope, that patriotism will stand for preventing a nuclear war.
- Hope, that self-reliance will become a virtue instead of a necessity.
- Hope, that love of others and a willingness to share what God has created on this earth; will allow free enterprise and democracy to flourish.

We need this hope. We need this religion. We need the main ingredient; "Give me, that old time religion!"

REFLECTIONS

I gazed into the puddle of water on the sidewalk after the rain. A mirror of reflections; the images as they floated on the water, was a reminder of the mirror of life.

A life, that constantly changes like the waves of the water. Evoking a wondering of what will be. Trying to find an answer to it all; resigned to clinging to thoughts.

It seems, that the closer hope comes into vision, the more elusive it becomes. How long will despair last; will it come to pass? Reflections that show hopes of happiness;

- Conversations of yesterday and what was;
- Today's Conversations and what is;
- Conversations of the future and what can be; and in the end, it is the reflections we see.

Looking Into the Mirror

I could see my reflection in the mirror. As I continued to look, I began to think about all the sad occurrences in my life. The missed opportunities, the promising ventures that I had started but never completed; what went wrong? I asked the person in the mirror, what went wrong. The response was very frank and to the point, "you have no acceptable excuses; you were given all the correct tools to get it done, to get it right; what happened?"

I could not answer the question. I could not generate a valid excuse. I simply stood there and continued to stare; questions racing through my head. Why am I here? Why was I born? What am I contributing to the wellness of mankind?

Still staring, I could not formulate an answer. I was beginning to feel uncomfortable about this person in the mirror, asking so many questions. I was becoming a bit irritated by the forcefulness, the constant pressing me for answers; this person was intimidating me! Out of anger and resentment, I managed the courage to shout at the image in the mirror.

I AM TIRED OF YOU LOOKING AT ME. I AM TIRED OF YOUR CONSTANT INTERROGATION OF ME. I AM SMARTER NOW. I HAVE LEARNED FROM THE LESSONS OF FAILURE IN LIFE. DO YOU HEAR ME? I WILL DO MY PART!

I will begin...to make beneficial contributions to the wellness of mankind.

Where I Live

Withering weeds
smothered under a partially fallen fence.
I hear sirens sighing, and brothers are dying.
I am so tired, of shots being fired;
and Junkies begging for a dime. Tell me...what is the time?

The breeze is growing colder,
winter seems to make things older; like a graying valley.
Clang! A trash can fell in the alley.
Starving rats, like vipers condensed in a vat.

My friends stay down this way, we never have a place to play;
so, we improvise and maximize.
Don't leave anything unlocked,
my house,
is in the next block!

FRIENDS

Where are they now?
The ones, who were willing to show me how.
Life has changed,
everything seems re-arranged.
Friends are supposed to be forever;
but people now, are oh so clever.
Talking smooth and indiscrete,
with lots of secrets to keep.

I remember in my youth;
the fairy would come to collect my tooth.
Fairytales and an Aesop's fable,
no one is willing to sit down at the table.
Memories of what was;
I loved you like you were my Cuz.
I remember when we were joined at the hip,
and nothing could make us flip.

Friends are supposed to be forever;
but people now, are oh so clever.
The ones who would show me how;
where are they now?

But We Keep On Goin Thru Changes!

The rabbit asked me,
"Have you ever seen a real Unicorn?"
"Well neither have I, but we keep on goin thru Changes,"
Can you tell me how?
"No, not now!"
"See what I mean, with your mind so keen;
but you have never seen...
a Unicorn."

"Just follow me,
and you will see; things you could not conceive,
hear stories you would not believe."
"Many will hurry to say, hey,
I would like to play.
Ends up, they must pay.
Changes!"

After being told; Being bold,
I followed the rabbit
down the hole.

I have been waiting since being born
to see the horse with one horn.
And I still ain't seen a Unicorn!
But we keep on goin thru changes.

Guilty Until Proven Innocent

Clang! Bang! The sound of steel doors slamming shut. It's a jail-house thang. But…I'm innocent. I did not do it! The swab-house theme that rings loud and clear; I didn't do it, sometimes comes with a tear.

I missed mama's funeral and then, uncle Jimmy died last week. My time keeps running, it never peaks. Got a letter from my gal today; she's stood by me through thick and thin. Saying; "don't worry baby," we are going to win. Visits are short and sweet… in here, I have no promises to keep. When I leave this window, my real life will rekindle. Watching my back on a daily basis…no

love is lost between the races. I try to occupy myself with all my might. It's a helluva thing, this freedom fight. I didn't do it, the swab-house theme that rings loud and clear.

It's my fear, that no one will hear, my wail...I want to be free of this jail. The starkness of the walls...the colors are drab in the halls. The coolness of steel.... how does it feel? To be stripped of a life of contribution, and now it is retribution. Years have come and gone, without so much as hearing a bird sing a song. My daughter had her baby girl this month; promised to bring her on the next visit...Man! They live so far away; I hate to see them always in transit.

My appeal is coming up; it is my last one, you know? But this time, it will be a show! After many lost battles to win my freedom, all I wanted to do was see God's kingdom; hear mighty sabers as they rattle. This will be an epic battle. My army is few, but we all knew...we live in a day; that has championed DNA.

As the gavel fell with a bang,
everybody sang and freedom rang.
Such a feeling of relief,
after years of suffering this grief.
I can never be compensated,
for life so abruptly abated.
It's a new world out there and so much has changed.
My life now must be re-arranged.
As I look at the beautiful blue sky above,
God has shown me His mercy and His love.
I didn't do it, is the swab-house theme that rings loud and clear.
I didn't do it...
Sometimes, comes with a tear.

Out Of The Closet Of My Mind

I am in a closet; it is dark inside,
but this is where I must reside;
and as you will find, the closet is in my mind.
No one will find me here, but then, that is my fear.
For so long, I have lived in this darkness.
The day is coming near; then again,
this is my fear.

I did not ask for this. It was not my wish.
But let the world have its way, today is the day.
I shall unlock this door and live in darkness no more.
I will come out into the light and fight the good fight.
Hoping for understanding; but this world is so demanding.

Will I be understood; or forced to live my life under a hood?
Will I be welcomed with open arms;
or will my life be threatened with cruelty and harm?
Will they give me some slack or discuss me behind my back?
No longer will I reside in this darkness.
I will face the world in all its starkness.
Lord knows, I have tried my best to hide...things inside.
But I want to be me; I long to be free. To be who I am!
What the world shall perceive, I no longer give a damn.

I am who I am!
A member of the human race; I too have a face.
As the locked door sounded a click and the brightness of the new light
went flick!
I shouted to the world today with glee... " at last; I am free!"

Future Shock

Little man sitting on the bench, the world viewing him
as a man devoid of intellectual sense.
As he feeds the pigeons, all he has left is his religion.
A look of sadness upon his face;
ex-communicated from the human race.
Due to his age, society would not allow him to turn the page,
of the book, containing his outlook.

As the pigeons meandered about his feet,
the hustle-bustle of this world continued its beat.
Hurry-scurry, going nowhere fast,
his world he knew, would not last.
His contributions were many, but nary a pat on the back if any.
He received his farewell gold watch…and truly it was fine;
and now all he can do, is watch the time.

Because of his age, they would not allow him to turn the page.
So here he sits full of anxiety;
well, so much said about society.

A man still capable of so many deeds;
now he sits despairingly, staring at the weeds.
With the pigeons meandering at his feet,
surely you too, can have a seat!

THE DESTINY OF MAN

Birth…
Out of the dark…come,
into the light.
Strange voices; mysterious visions.

Life…
My journey beckons, with forces unknown;
towards destiny…
I came with nothing;

Death...
Dust, the destiny of man.
I leave with nothing.

IMAGINATION

Already, my imagination wants to take wing and soar through your mind, searching and seeking the unknown. Such questions as to when, where, why and how, dominate my thoughts, in my dreams, you are there to stay,

But I woke up today,
When my mind began to play.
Wondering when; wondering where,
me it would decide to send.
My imagination conjured you up, flick!
Is this just another elusive trick?
The air is so sweet and fresh.
And you, like golden petals on a new spring dress.
Hi!
I thought of you today.
And visions of bright sunshine and radiant joy and laughter,
abounded within my mind.

Imagining You Here

Imagining you near
Whispering in your ear…
In the cool of the night;
The flames of loves embers so bright.
Loving you seems so right.
Only you will know,
Under the flickering flames of the fires warm glow;
That I love you so.
Water cannot quench the thirst,
Of a love unlike the first.
Like no love before,
I only want you more.
Beneath the flames of the fire,
It is you that I desire.
And only you will know,
That I love you so.

So Many Questions, Now Isn't That Strange?

Is it time for my learning to begin?
Is it that period of life I am dying to see?
Is it that period that once began,
And now, is relived again?
Did anything change? Was anything strange?
Cause life revolves, regardless of resolves.
This world continues to turn, as we continue to learn.
Yearning for knowledge,
Some things just are not taught in college.
And if you remember, time is indeed but a number.
Either Time moving forward, or time is standing still,
It is a period in life that demands will.
Will I instigate?
Will I investigate?
Will I yearn?
Will I Learn?
So many questions;
Nothing will ever change,
Now isn't that strange?

THE WOMAN IN RED

From a distance I saw her...she floated across the room. As I gazed, it was as if I had just seen the most beautiful ruby in the world. For only a moment, our eyes met. Dressed in that ruby-red dress, she dazzled! Making my way through the crowd trying to move closer, I could not resist, I had to know her.

I inched slowly forward in her direction. Sometimes she would disappear in the crowd. But to my relief, she would suddenly reappear. Still making my way through the crowd, I could see her no more. She had simply vanished! I searched in vain but she was no more. Where could she have gone? Who was she?

I quickly ran outside, hoping she had opted for a breath of fresh air; or a little time to gather her thoughts. But she was no more. Disappointedly I slowly walked backed inside, constantly glancing over my shoulder, hoping she would be there. As I continued to walk back across the room, my mind whirling I thought; Tonight, when I go to bed, I will dream about this room; where for the first time in my life,

I saw the woman in red;
who will forever
be in my head.

My Muse

Inspires my creative desires;
my muse,
a true daughter of Zeus.
Imaginations soar,
inspirations roar;
feeling I need to be, that other side of me.
That wants to write,
about the fight,
for a love facing cessation.
About dying embers, losing their glow.
Yet, you are the inspiration that drives the writing;
of the lines that seem to intertwine,
with the reinvigorated embers that glow in my mind.
That wants to create the art, that inspires me to be a part
of a love supreme; a love seldom seen.
My muse,
makes me want to be, that other side of me.

I Want To Know Your Name

My words ring true, thru and thru, I really want to know you.
How was your day, busy, busy, in a busy way?
My day is going swell, and life is treating you well, this I can tell.
And that smile, will linger,
for a while in my mind;until a way to capture it, I find.
I have found you! But the question is, have you found me too?
I want to know your name.
Who are you and what are you about? What accolades can you tout?
Are you the woman in red dancing in my head?
A fairytale read before I go to bed?
Are you, my fear? My fear of becoming vulnerable;
my fear, of the key that may unlock my heart; my fear, of a fresh start?
Are you the beautiful flower of spring,

the mighty thunder that makes the sky ring,
the magnificent oak that reaches for the sky;
or simply, a fixation in my mind, soon to say goodbye?
Who are you?
Are you the canary in the cage;
who when the door is open, is afraid to engage?
Longing for freedom of expression;
tired of traveling the road of regression.
Longing to be listened to and
be truly cherished for who you are, to be someone's star;
Forever giving from a heart, that is true.
Like the songs you sing, sweet harmonies ring.
I want to know your name!
Did I fail to introduce myself?
Excuse me, let me place my vanity on a shelf.
I am, the man without the glam. The man who will stand by you
when circumstances come to try you.
Who will be by your side when there is no place to hide.
Since love is fleeting, it is not part of this meeting.
I like you for who you are; you, are my rising star!

The Blossom of Spring

*T*he coldness of winter has loosened its grip…and the warming wind of spring flows through the air. A warmth that indicates what is to come. Inspiring an awakening of newness; of life and love. Life and love have awakened with a new energy that cannot be contained. So powerful. that even having been covered over by the remnants of winter, nothing can prevent its emergence. It is only fitting that my love for you has been invigorated.

Love bells ring,
like the birds in my heart sing.
A love so true, longing to be with you.

I want to hold and caress you in my arms
and unlock all of your charms.
I want to kiss you gently; capturing your love,
you submit unrelentingly.

This love is true, meant only for you.
You are the blossom of my spring,
and it is you, who makes my heart sing!

MY HEART SINGS

It is you that has awakened a heart that now sings,
a song of life, a song of joy.
My heart roars like the wind
during a violent storm.
My love will protect you from harm.

In you I have found a friend; only our hearts together can comprehend.
For you, my love will never end.
When I think of you, I must say;
with your heart, I will never play.
Love is not a game to be played,
through love, one cannot simply wade.

My heart sings.
It sings; I love you, love you,
over and over again.
My life will never be the same.
Into my life; I am so glad you came.

The Event

My little caterpillar slowly crawled across the leaf. Looking, searching for that special place. Too much energy had been spent searching. My little caterpillar was weary. It needed a place to rest, a place to gather strength for the upcoming event.

My caterpillar was very fuzzy. Its hairs and body moved with a wave-like motion. Upon reaching its chosen destination, it started to build the protective shelter that would keep it safe. It labored day and night. Until, finally it was wrapped securely within the walls of its cocoon. Now, it felt safe and warm; from the outside world, it felt protected from harm.

Safe in its protective shell, it fell asleep. Sleep that would bring it closer to the upcoming event. What an event it would be! My little caterpillar was determined to show those that had mocked its slowness, that had laughed at its seemingly lack of purpose and direction. Yes, it would show them all the power of beauty; the power of patience. Time for my caterpillar was non-existent. As time passed, the cocoon developed hairline cracks. The force of what was inside could not be contained. The walls of the cocoon exploded! My little caterpillar that had retreated into its self-imposed prison (cocoon), suddenly reappeared to the world.

Now, it was no longer a fuzzy, slow-moving creature. It had transformed into a thing of grace and beauty with colors beyond compare. It now moved through life as a graceful movement of life itself. My little caterpillar was now a beautiful butterfly!

Such is the story of our love. Our love has transformed from the insecure slowness of life into something beautiful. Our love blossomed much like the very flowers that this butterfly will visit. Our love will never retreat from the world for the safety of a cocoon. Our love emerged and will continue to blossom and be a love of beauty. A love that has purpose and intent, our love is "the Event!"

You Mean The World To Me

This is just to say,
without you, it's been a lonely day;
and hey baby, you mean the world to me.

Missing your laughter during the day;
missing those silly games, we sometimes play.
You know, I want to touch you.
Right now!
You know, I want to love you.
Right now!
Feel my love growing warmer. Feel my love.

I think if there is a thing called happiness, I have found it in you;
and hey baby, you mean the world to me.

I Can't Tell You Why

Loving you so much…
I just want to fly, High in the sky.
I can't tell you why;
just love you I must.
Love you the way, I Love you today.
Is it that you feel…close and so real?
I can't tell you why your heart is my smile,
or why I want to be with you for more than a while.
My love for you is such, I long to feel your touch.
You mean more to me…more than I can see.
Envisioning us frolicking in a field of Heather,
we were destined to be together.
As water rushes from a fountain, we can climb any mountain,
I will always love you;
"I can't tell you why."

If I Give You My Heart, What Will You Do With It?

I give you my heart…
hoping, from you it never parts.
Treasure it with all that is within you
and never let go, of a heart that continues to grow.

For grow it will, until the earth stands still.
It is fragile and oh, so humble.
Never, let it fall or stumble.
It is forever giving, to keep our love living.

Hold this heart in your hands and feel it,
hold it in your hands and caress it,
hold it in your hands and kiss it.
Hold it onto your heart and love it.

Then you will see,
that if you give your heart to me,
a love like none other will await thee.
Take my heart of love beyond compare;
to you I give,
the love of a heart so rare.

The Little Leaf that Fell to Love

This is a story about a love secured. It is a story of emergence into the changing seasons; not knowing what is to come; not knowing if the elements would erode the very fabric of life sustained. She had tasted life and the sensations of being attached to life itself (her stalk), but she could hold on no longer. It was time to give up. She could not contain her secret any longer. What she held inside, hidden from all eyes, was guarded ever so carefully. Her secret was soon to be exposed. She had to let go.

The life she had known, the security of her stalk, seemed forever lost. She wondered about the life that awaited her. What would she do? What should she do? She had but one choice. A choice that she knew she had to face. Knowing that she still had life yet within her, but weakening quickly, she could hold on no longer.... she let go.

Dropping gently from her stalk of life, falling and spiraling in slow motion as she floated downward, she fell into the hand of love. She

landed in the hand of tenderness, a hand of humility, a hand that would soothe and caress the cares of the world away. she landed into the gentle hand of love that would offer new life with purpose.

When she fell, she felt strange; her colors had changed! She could hide it no longer. Her secret, her true colors, were now exposed for all to see. Colors so radiant and beautiful, they were a pleasure for the eyes to behold. Still full of life, her transformation was a joy to the soul.

The hand that would forever hold her will never close. The hand that holds her now will never squeeze her life….so delicate is she. The hand that holds her now will never stop loving the beauty of her colors.

Like a dove,
a little leaf fell from above.
Into a waiting hand, a little leaf fell to love.
Into a hand spattered with rain,
to bring comfort once again.

In a hand that is strong and giving,
my little leaf will keep on living.
My little leaf that fell from above,
will be forever loved.

Dwelling Thoughts

Is there really any love?
For many, there is never the first time...
others think of the last.
Strolling through the remnants of my mind,
I find fragments of past affairs, ribbons, smiles, cards, promises.
Unfinished sentences, misplaced nouns;
hoping for something that can never be.
Blindness is contagious.
Everyone looks but they cannot see;
the real me.

Here I am!
Inside this human form;
this thing man calls body.
Can't you hear me? I am shouting,
"I want out"!
I am nothing you can hold, nor can you see.
You must feel me;
like a breath of autumn breeze, like a quick beat of your heart.
Wonder about me.
Wonder!
Then, I can continue to exist.
Even if it is just a figmentation, of your imagination.

Continuing Thoughts

Yes, there is love.
The first can be the last.
Can we say to love is to live;
when there is so much agony and pain?
I hear the voices... As they resound more clearly at each calling.
They seem to be pulling me ever so slightly into a web of emotion.
Sometimes they cry, "I want out".
I feel myself resisting the voices...I'm confused.
The voices are louder now, more distinct.
My ears take on a visual transition.
Yes, I see you...you want out.
Darkness surrounds me; my world.
I find myself fumbling. Groping, reaching out;
are you there?
Darkness; Voices screaming now,
I want out, out, out!
Bumping into objects unfamiliar to my sensitive touch.
Help! I'm falling. Are you there?
Please come into me.
Please help me to see...the real me.

BUT I WAS AFRAID

Today, I really wanted to talk to you.
But I was afraid.
So much I want to say,
So much I need to say.
Its hell keeping it all inside.
The flames of the fire,
Burning with the desire,
To call out and shout.
But I was afraid.
I needed you then,
I had no other friend.
But…
You were afraid.

THINGS SAID

The things said today,
will they go away?
Are they here to stay?
Who's to say?

Hanging on to a love that is gone,
where did it all go wrong?
A slip of the tongue,
looking at my hands tender from being wrung.

What I said cannot be taken back; that power I lack.
Now I dread, the things I said.
It is all in my head…
the things I said.

Make Up Your Mind

Learning and yearning
Sometimes I think I am sane.
Sometimes I think I am vain.
I want to stay, then again,
I want to go away!
I Cannot, make up my mind today.
People surround me,
they just will not let me be.
Cannot seem to understand, why they cannot see...me.
I want to stay, then again,
I want to go away!
I Cannot,
seem to make up my mind today.

Running Away to Love

Today I packed my bags; some of my clothes were rags.
It was because my life is not the same. and it was time for change.
I determined; it is time to leave this place. There are things I must face.
Still, it is time to leave this place.
I will go to a place where I can start to relieve my heart.
Too many memories remain,
I am determined not to relive them again.
Nothing will ever be the same.
No longer will I gaze through the windowpane,
staring blankly at the rain.
I am determined not to relive this again.
I will need food for this trip, to not be fed, my heart will rip.
I must prepare.
Food for the soul is what I need. The words of others, I will not heed.
What do they know? Only that I must go,
to that place that will feed my soul.
Wow! My thinking is very bold.
Do I dare, or do I continue to stare,
at the fallen rain, upon the windowpane?
No! It is time to leave this place. I will fight for my life as I should.
Only if I would; "You know what", I think I should.
I shall run away.
What more can I say?
I packed my bags and yes, some of my clothes are rags.
I am running away to love today and
that is where I will stay!

The Picture

Your photograph sits on the table, your face framed in all its beauty.
As I gaze upon you, our eyes meet.
When I look into your eyes, it is you I see,
And I know our love will be.

My heart skips a beat. I want our love to repeat.
I see the sky, and I know why,
There is so much I want to show

Your smile bathes me like the morning sun,
Makes my heart run.
For us, there is no darkness; we will be together soon.
Finding each other by the brightness of the moon.

I see heaven
And feel as lucky as the number seven.
I know it is you I want to kiss; I know it is you I miss.
Because, when I look into your eyes,
I thank God above.
And I know for sure,
It is you that I love.

MISSING YOU

I wanted to write you a letter,
but for some reason, I thought leaving this message would be better.
To say what I feel and let it be real.
So much I want to say,
but I am, having difficulty finding the way.
I don't know? I just want it to flow.
Let the words, fall as they may;
all I know, is that I feel love for you today.
I miss you.

I cannot afford to use the word love loosely,
but love is welling up inside of me profusely.
I try to contain myself.
Is it because I feel that I need to maintain myself?
So as not to expose what I cannot seem to hide,
because it is deep inside.
I don't know? I just love you so.
Days have gone by without hearing your voice;
Without me making a choice.
The quiet conversation I now have with myself,
sitting here alone staring at the walls; makes me realize
that I must come out of this hell. I know you can tell.
I need you, fool that I am; realization now that you are gone.
Compromise if you will, because I love you still;
I miss you!

THE DISCOVERY

One day I discovered,
that I indeed loved her.
Some say that love is blind, but it is only to remind;
us to open our eyes. So, we can see,
the discovery!
With eyes wide open,
It is clear to see through the friction, that this love is not fiction.
It is real, something you can feel.
Are emotions so damaged. that they cannot heal?
To be contained internally, under a tight seal.
Remove the seal and begin to see,
the discovery!
Someday,
she will discover, that I truly love her.

How Could I Have Ever Let You Go?

We are sitting here with the lights turned down low.
The wine glasses are sparkling in the subdued light.
The fragrance of the wine on the table drifts into our nostrils;
the sweet smell of wine.
With the music low and soothing,
we slowly move into a world of love.
You are close; I have my arms around your waist,
never wanting to let you go.
I whisper into your ear "Honey I love you."
You smile gently, as only you can smile.
A sense of security and relaxation overcomes us now.
You tilt your head back and gaze into my eyes;
"I love you", you say.
Drunk with love I say to you,
"I will never let you go".
I am, sitting here with the lights turned down low;
still wanting to know, how could I have ever,
let you go?

BACK TOGETHER?

Was it fate or circumstances that brought us back together?
To try again to master those things, we thought we could weather.
Some things we learned, but then again,
some things were burned.
Feelings were hurt and suspicions remain,
Will our love ever be the same?
Collateral damage from the past,
Some of loves' embers did not last.
Still full of elation, we proceeded to build a new foundation.
One that would withstand the onslaught,
Not realizing it was all for naught.
The scars of the past lay upon the embers of our love,
We really do not fit like a glove.
There is however, one thing we can defend;
In each other,
we will always have a friend.

A Rose May Whither And Die

I remember the day my rose appeared with its beautiful face of color. From a small protrusion on the stalk that held it, it had developed into a young bud. It had burst into life with energy and promise. A promise of gifting the garden where it resided, with the fragrance of life.

As the days passed, the bud grew into a beautiful rose. As a gentle breeze passed through the garden, I could smell a sweet perfume, its' scent lingering in the air. The smell of its powerful fragrance was beckoning me closer. It shone with brilliance as it bathed in the sunlight. It was so beautiful and fragrant, I had to possess it!

I gently snipped it from its stem and placed it into the finest vase I could find. It was so precious and beautiful, I had to possess it! I fed it the cool water of life, hoping it would never deny me the pleasure of smelling its fragrance, a fragrance that contained love and hope. But a captured rose has a life that is fleeting, and as the days waned by, my rose began to die.

> *Each day, as its petals fought to maintain,*
> *it was all in vain.*
> *No matter how much the cool water tried,*
> *my rose withered and died.*
> *With a life so fleeting,*
> *I was happy to have had my chance meeting.*
> *The fragrance of my rose is here to stay;*
> *the fragrance of my rose, it never goes away!*

With This Ring

With this ring I be-wed,
until we are parted as the dead.
That is what we said.

The next day, all we did was play.
Making plans, the world was in our hands.
Thinking of creating a family, trying our best to avoid calamity.
But try as we might,
somewhere along the line we lost the fight.
Fingers pointed; the connection is now disjointed.
Falling apart at the seams, trying to hold on by any means.
Our ways have parted; look at what we started.

With this ring I be-wed,
until we were parted as the dead.
That is what we said!
Neither of us died; who is to say someone lied?
No one died...but somebody,
cried.

You Know, Sometimes Go By

Sometimes go by...you forgot to say hi.
Sometimes are such...
You forgot that much needed touch.
You forgot that sweet day in the park...
Your memory seems a bit dark.

You know sometimes birds' land...
You forgot to hold her hand...
Let her know that you are her man.

Sometimes let...you forget.
Sometimes burn like embers...
Sometimes you remember.
Sometimes are such...You forgot that much.
You know sometimes go by...
I wonder why?

The Land of Hummingbirds and Butterflies

My love for you is composed by nature
and nature is beauty within itself;
a cascading waterfall, a budding flower,
glistening dew on the morning grass, or a starlit sky.

I envision hummingbirds and butterflies when I think of you,
your beauty stands out like the beautiful patterns
that adorn the butterfly.
Your beauty glistens like the flitting hummingbird
under the morning sun,
each being so different; such is your love.
In the land of hummingbirds and butterflies,
lives a love that beats in my heart.
Racing like the hummingbird,
in search of another flower, to savor the sweet nectar of life.
Like the butterfly adorned in beautiful colors,
moving effortlessly, from flower to flower;
it is as if beauty attracts beauty.

My love for you cries;
I will always be there waiting for your love,
in the land of hummingbirds and butterflies.

In Case You Were Wondering

To Whom it may Concern,

It is my hope this letter finds you in good spirits and of good cheer. I wish you were near. I am sending you this letter, to let you know without doubt, what this is all about. This letter is all I have to show, but it will help to let you know.

Today, I received A Letter to Myself concerning coming to grips with my life, as well as The Main Ingredient. I need a belief system other than the distorted images and the Reflections I see while Looking into The Mirror. There are lingering thoughts about my environment and Where I Live. Remembering my Friends; It was a struggle back then, we all wanted to win. But We Keep on Goin' Thru Changes! Somewhere things got off track; trying to get my life back. They say, you are Guilty Until Proven Innocent; even if you didn't do it. Time to get Out of the Closet of My Mind and face the Future Shock of my inevitable appointment with The Destiny of Man.

My Imagination will not allow me to stop Imagining You Here. I have So Many Questions, Now Isn't That Strange? Are you The Woman in Red dancing in my head? I envision you as My Muse; an element of intrigue; I Want to Know Your Name. The Blossom of Spring, is why My Heart Sings; about The Event that lets you know why You Mean the World to Me. Try as I may, I must say, I Can't Tell You Why. But If I Give You My Heart, What Will You Do with It? Will you hold me like The Little Leaf That Fell to Love?

I have these Dwelling Thoughts, that turn into Continuing Thoughts. I wanted to share them, But I Was Afraid. When I did speak, there were Things Said that I dread; that only helped you to Make Up Your Mind. The decision was made; you were Running Away to Love. Now, all I have is The Picture of you, which reminds me, why I am Missing You. Faced with The Discovery that I love you so; asking myself over and over again, How Could I Have Ever Let You Go. We trekked through stormy weather and eventually got Back Together. But hard as we tried, we both knew that A Rose May Wither and Die. We now have memories of With This Ring I Be-wed; that is what we said! Sometimes Go By, I wonder why? Even though we shared goodbyes, I will always be there waiting for your love, In the Land of Hummingbirds and Butterflies.

Sincerely Yours,

The Author

Artist and writer Michael Loyd Rogers was born in St. Louis, Missouri. He now resides in Houston, Texas. Rogers' artistry journey started at an early age: as a child, he attained his first bicycle by entering a drawing contest for kids; with the first prize being the bicycle. An avid outdoor type, he has a love for animals and nature.. A deep fascination with life and perception drives his artistry; to him, everything created has purpose; finding that purpose, is the challenge.

A military veteran (US Air Force), his writing started after his return from the Vietnam War. Although he has been writing for several years, Rogers has never published his works in the form of a book. He now presents his first book for the world of poetry.

His writing paints a vividly poignant and at the same time joyful portrait of life for the reader. Winner of two previous awards for two of the writings in this collection, his connection to nature and the human element of emotion, is evident in the manner he weaves a story.

Utilizing a blend of essay, prose and poetry, his book sets the stage with, A Letter to Myself; illuminating thoughts of coming into oneself; and the ins and outs of love. He prepares the reader for a journey on the road to the circle of life; where at the fork in the road we must choose which road we will take. In case you were wondering, he closes the curtains with a letter of patience and hope; Rogers will place you forever inside a portrait of life.

www.ingramcontent.com/pod-product-compliance
Lightning Source LLC
Chambersburg PA
CBHW080348170426
43194CB00014B/2728